The author has done BA in public relations with honors and masters in Islamic history and civilization.

He is currently working in space and astronomy field and has published scientific researches.

He has also studied professional trainer making from Canadian Academy for Development & Training and American Global Training Board.

He holds an international training practice license.
The author is also a reader and pianist.

To the spirit of our great lost scholar… he is not forgotten.

To the person who taught countless people in the East and the West.

To the pioneer of human resource development sciences in our Arab world.

To the compassionate father and respectable educator.

To our professor and our scholar, Dr. Ibrahim al-Faqi, may Allah be pleased with him.

We send our faithful prayers asking Allah to grant you Paradise.

Abdulhadi Taqi

BE UNIQUE

AUSTIN MACAULEY PUBLISHERS™
LONDON • CAMBRIDGE • NEW YORK • SHARJAH

ISBN – 9789948844129 – (Paperback)
ISBN – 9789948452751 – (E-Book)

Application Number: MC-10-01-6633729
Age Classification: E

First Published (2021)
AUSTIN MACAULEY PUBLISHERS FZE
Sharjah Publishing City
P.O Box [519201]
Sharjah, UAE

www.austinmacauley.ae
+971 655 95 202

To each one who encouraged and urged me to write…
And everyone who had an influence on my life, either negative or positive.

My appreciation is also for those who encouraged me to have the passion for writing:

My mother
My father

Dr. Ibrahim Al-Faqi
The writer, Noura Al-Rowaiy.

Hope is my title, knowledge is my weapon, and the light
is my sanctuary.

– Abdulhadi Taqi

Introduction

Welcome, you precious readers. Let's begin a long and wide journey into the world of Dr. Ibrahim al-Faqi. Let's dive deep into the gist of his experience and effort throughout his life, especially the positive energy and philosophy of which he held the secrets, which was apparent from his work.

We live in a world in which survival is only for the strongest. If you are not strong enough in life, you will fail to survive amongst the strong. Therefore, you must learn, train, and make changes and developments. You must make progress regularly and benefit from your experiences and mistakes and also from the experiences and mistakes of others, as we must benefit from others not only from ourselves.

Many years ago, Dr. Ibrahim al-Faqi founded a very vital science—Human Resource Development—which has become a registered brand and has captured the admiration of people around the world. It is designed around the essential human desires which are represented in his permanent search to improve himself and to continuously upgrade to what is better.

In this book, I will tackle the most important sayings of Dr. Ibrahim al-Faqi and give a brief explanation with what I have deduced from these sayings and thoughts. There are fifty sayings, and I will discuss each one separately. Hence, these are some of the experiences, experiments, research projects, and meaningful thoughts that I bring to you to enrich your soul. These sayings will not only add new information in your minds and selves, but also will help you to rid yourselves of the delusions that have hindered you to reach your capabilities and the glory of your divine formation that Allah the

Almighty gifted you with. Indeed, there are no individuals who are to be called failures; there are only those who label themselves as such.

If you are ready to learn about an important matter in your life and realize the importance of your own self, let's take this step by step with a firm positive attitude and an insightful eye that will see till the end.

The Biography of Dr. Ibrahim Al-Faqi

Dr. Ibrahim Mohamed al-Sayed al-Faqi was born in Abo al-Namras village, in al-Monib district, in al-Giza governorate. He won the tennis championship in Egypt several times. In addition, he represented the Egyptian official team at the World Table Tennis Championship in West Germany, in 1969.

In terms of professional life, he joined the ranks of the hotel sector manager at the Palestine Hotel in Alexandria and then reached the third degree at the age of 25.

Afterwards, he emigrated to Canada to study management and started there from scratch, where he began to work as a dish washer, then as a guard for a restaurant, then a chair and table porter in a hotel, until finally he became one of the most prominent Arab pioneers in the field of philosophy, besides being the founder of the science of Human Resources Development.

The Journey of Dr. Ibrahim Al-Faqi

Dr. Ibrahim al-Faqi worked at an institute for hotels in Egypt in the seventies and received his first salary of 25 piasters.

You cannot imagine the degree of happiness that the doctor felt, after much fatigue, when he got his first paycheck. When you are rewarded for your work, after getting tired from it, you will naturally feel very happy. How about if you feel this feeling from the very first paycheck, even if your salary is very low!

Obviously, the idea of travel had been in Dr. Ibrahim's mind since he had started working in hotels. He was constantly looking for the best. If we are not ambitious, there will be no remarkable progress in our lives.

Dr. Ibrahim al-Faqi got all of his practical experience in Egypt, as he worked in restaurants and hotels and learned English and French. He was preparing himself for travel and for reaching a better tomorrow, full of hope. He was also making other achievements, such as his award for the table tennis championship and winning the title of Egypt's champion in table tennis. Dr. Ibrahim used to say, "Make excellence within yourself, and do not wait for excellence to come knock on your door."

In 1978, Dr. Al-Faqi emigrated to Canada, where his first salary was $1.50 per hour—a very small amount, but he was very happy with this amount. In fact, many of us lack satisfaction, patience, and optimism. These three characteristics were the cause of the doctor's happiness, even in the face of many obstacles. His journey started from the first night when he was looking for work and was wondering,

"What is the easiest job? What is the hardest job?" He was anticipating the prospect of having the best job in the field.

It is not important where the person starts; but what matters is where the person ends up. They told him to be a dishwasher, so he accepted this. He did not think negatively about the job or say, "What is this job?!" or "I graduated from hotel university. I've learned two languages!" For him, this was the beginning of reaching senior management.

Remarkably, the journey went on with great challenges. As they wanted someone experienced, he was unfortunately fired three times. Each time he went to a new place he was expelled from it. But on these three occasions, he learned new things and gained beneficial experience. This is what Dr. Al-Faqi opted to convey to the people: If you want a job, ask yourself, initially, "What does my job require? Do my qualifications meet with the job requirements? What can I do in this job?"

In fact, the journey was so long for Dr. Al-Faqi. He worked in restaurants, worked as a guard at night, worked on the railways, and worked in various fields, so long as the work would not be dissatisfactory to Allah, until he received his college diploma in Canada. Moreover, he graduated with an excellent degree with honors.

After that, he worked on a series of studies and research projects, worked and worked, reaped expertise, and then, within eight years, he became the first Egyptian-Arab-Muslim general manager to receive this status in Canada.

The Best of Words

15

In this book, we will pick from every orchard of wisdom. This man has rendered a collection of wise sayings, values, and advice, which he has offered to every person who wishes to live a better life and to achieve all his dreams. Thus, I am going to speak briefly about each statement.

Call for Satisfaction with What Allah Has Predestined:

"We see what we do not want; we want what we do not see. Therefore, we lose the value of what we see, and get lost in the mirage of what we do not see, so be careful not to lose the value of what you see."

Sometimes we do not appreciate the value of something except when we lose it. We do not feel the value of that thing while it is with us, but when we lose it, we feel as if we have lost the whole world. My friend's grandfather used to blame him too much, and my friend was constantly complaining about his grandfather's mistreatment. Suddenly, when his grandfather died, he felt a great loss. He was crying all day and night. In addition, he was saying to me, "I wish I could correct what I said to you about my grandfather. Indeed, my life without him is meaningless!"

In fact, the instinct of human beings is to renew, but we should also be satisfied with what Allah has destined for us and say, "Praise be to Allah."

Call for Understanding the Life:

"Without the existence of the opposite meaning, the meaning would be meaningless."

Verily, if there was no existence of the opposite meaning, we would not have been able to differentiate between the good and the evil. In addition, we would not be able to make decisions in our lives, as there is both positive and negative meaning for what surrounds us. Thus, we must follow the positive path. When we see bad companions and good ones and see the difference between their deeds, we will find the best deeds and meanings with the good ones. Perhaps we will hang out with the wrong people for a while, and this is known as the learning period, as all of us can fall into mistakes, but this does not mean failure. However, the continuity of doing wrongs is failure itself.

Henry Ford said, "Failure is the opportunity that allows you to start over with greater intelligence."

"Were it not for my challenges, I would not have learned, and had it not been for my suffering, I would not have had a good life. If I had not become ill, I would not have been in good health. If it were not for my poverty, I would not have had wealth, and if it had not been for my loss, I would not have succeeded. Indeed, were it not for my realizing, I would not be the person that I am now."

When we look at the words of Dr. Al-Faqi, we see that the content of them is similar throughout his speeches. We can glean from his words that life is based on our experiences and that experiences benefit us. Failure is the threshold of success, and the word "failure" cannot be found in Al-Faqi's dictionary.

Through his beautiful saying, "We learn from everything that passes through our lives. We learn from every minute passing through us. And we learn from the negatives to achieve success." If I had the chance to complete this statement of Al-Faqi with an added phrase, I would write, "Without my failures, I wouldn't have established my pillars of success."

When your arrow fails to hit its target, do not think about the mistake that you've made, but instead drag the second arrow, and think, "What should I do to properly hit the target this time?"

"What seemed painful at first, I found it comfortable. What seemed saddening, I found it joyful. Moreover, what seemed difficult, I found easy, what seemed to be failure, I found in it lies success. What seemed dark, I found it bright. And I learned not to look at things from a superficial point of view."

Dr. Al-Faqi often repeats his saying, "Without existence of the opposite meaning, the meaning would be meaningless." Al-Faqi sees that the pain of yesterday has come to rest and the sorrow of yesterday has become joy, and the difficulty has turned into ease. In addition, the darkness has turned into light and brightness, and things must not be viewed in a negative way, as they correct the path of our lives and from them we glean knowledge.

Edison completed more than a thousand experiments before reaching success. Then he invented the lamp and lit up the whole world.

Thus, the beginning of every success is failure, the beginning of all rest is pain, and the beginning of all light is darkness.

Do not regret the beginning, because it will vanish. However, take more care of the end, because it will last.

I conclude by saying that for each beginning there is an end. Therefore, have the best endings and do not despair!

"Life is only a hope accompanied by pain and surprised by death."

Ibrahim al-Faqi divided life into three words: hope, pain, and predestined death.

Surely, if we contemplate on these words, we will find that they describe life. All human beings thrive on hope. Life does not go on without pain. And eventually we will be surprised by the end of our lives.

Live your life on hope, expect good, adapt yourself to be optimistic, define your ends and goals, and work on accomplishing them in a perfect way.

If you feel pain, be ready for it, and know that if Allah loves a worshiper, he will inflict him/her. Therefore, face these obstacles and challenges fiercely, trust in Allah, and remain steadfast in your plight, as Allah the Almighty said in Surah al-Baqarah [2:153]: **Indeed Allah is with the patient.**

Remember that your reward will not be lost.

When death comes, this is the truth of the world, and every soul will taste death. All human beings will meet this fate. Therefore, live sincerely for Allah the Almighty and live with good morals. Bring a smile to the face of others, and treat them always as if that will be the last time you see them. Incite others to pray for you, not against you, after your departure. Try to get closer to Allah. In this moment, you will feel that your path of life is full of brightness.

And finally, you must understand life to be able to learn to live happily.

"Life is a fantastic novel. You should read every line of it till the end. Never stop on a sad line. Perhaps the end is beautiful."

— **Mohammed al-Shawaf**

Remember Always:

"Live every moment as if it is the last one in your life, live with belief in Allah and adherence to the morals and Sunnah of the Prophet, peace and blessings be upon him. Live with hope, with love, with struggling, and appreciate the value of life."

Many people do not appreciate the value of being alive. One can see many of the people neglecting the worship of Allah, heading towards the pleasures of the world, and many of them are too arrogant and miserly to even smile in the face of their Muslim brothers. Then, when Allah inflicts him/her with a malignant disease, or any disease actually, you see a remarkable change in his/her personality. Noticeably, he/she draws closer to Allah, treats people well again, and regrets what he/she was doing before. Here is the question: why did you get yourself into this terrible situation?

Live each moment as if it is the last one. Do not wait for an infliction in order to change and correct your life path. Be afraid that Allah may take your soul at any time and you will not have the chance again to do good! Start from today by doing good and dealing with all people with kindness. Take a step closer to Allah, and you will find that the darkness turns to light. Follow the morals of the Prophet, peace and blessings be upon him, as he provided us with moral lessons and wisdom in dealing with life. He is the best role model for all mankind. Remember that whoever plants good among the people, Allah plants all the good upon his path of life.

Live with hope. It is said that the human being can live 40 days without food, four days without water, four minutes without air, but it is impossible to live four seconds without hope, as it is the key to all of the closed doors.

Live with love—the love of Allah, our Prophet (peace and blessings be upon him), your parents, yourself, your family, the people, the creatures, and good deeds.

"Where there is love, there is life," Gandhi said.

Appreciate the value of life, the value of the freedom that you have, the value of food, drink, shelter, health, and the blessings that Allah has gifted to you.

Many people in Africa suffer from a lack of provision. Even in the countries with many technological advances, the youth are homeless and have no shelter to protect them from the cold. Praise be to Allah for the blessing of Islam and the unity of the family.

You are currently writing the story of your own life, minute by minute. So, make it a story worthy to be read.

A Call for Abandoning Bad Habits:

"There are things, people, and even parts that go with us on our life journey for a particular reason and for a specified period of time, but not for all the journey. Therefore, it is the time to leave them alone."

Dr. Al-Faqi was speaking in this quote of the opportunists who come into your life during a certain period and stay only for a specific purpose. You may encounter them during the study period to cheat from your test. They will abuse your efforts then disappear after school.

Try to ignore this type of person as much as possible—the one who wants you for a purpose or service, not for the sake of love, but only for the sake of getting benefits from you, while you are exerting much effort and wasting your time on him.

Is this person worthy of continuing the journey of life with you?

The answer is: no! You should not allow yourself to be abused by others. You have the dignity to get away from this bad type of person.

"Our life is busy with unessential disagreements, because our minds are full of unessential ideas and thoughts. As a result, we are leading a meaningless life. In fact, it is an unessential one."

Verily, this is a big problem in the Arab World, as some believe that they have to disagree with others and discuss their issues in an impulsive way! Even if he is wrong, he insists that he is the only one who can be right, even if the subject of the argument is superficial. His thought process revolves only around the idea of disagreeing, as if he were created for this sake. The terrible thing is that he always thinks he is right and never falls into error. In fact, he does not know or understand anything! As a result of bad habits, you have convinced yourself to think negatively. Therefore, abandon the bad habits, and adhere to the positive ones and the habits that will make others admire you. Live a meaningful life.

"When we blame others, we become their victims. We start to justify our actions towards them, and then they steal a part of our precious life which might be the last moment."

If you truly care about your friend, who in turn does not care about you and is not concerned about you, do not go to him and blame him. Do not make your misery or happiness dependent on a person or a friend, or even a loved one. Make your happiness and sadness dependent upon Allah, because Allah hears you whenever you call to him, and He responds to your call. Allah the Almighty set aside a specified time for you to pray to Him and communicate with Him, and there is a direct relationship between psychological comfort and closeness to Allah. The closer you are to Allah, the more your psychological comfort increases. Indeed, the most beautiful moment is the moment of worship.

Caring for those who do not care for you is an offense.

"Do not ignite a fire that you are unable to extinguish."

Do not talk of things that you are ignorant about, because you will start a war which is going to gradually escalate, and then you will not be able to extinguish its raging fire.

Thus, stay away from negativity. Frequent negative talk sets a fire! Unfortunately, our community often talks about cons and rarely talks about pros! They argue in trivial matters that they do not need to talk about, such as politics and religion. Therefore, leave these two areas to the scholars and experts.

You must think before you speak, and remember that your good words are a beautiful fragrance. Try to spread this fine fragrance.

"Stay away from people who try to belittle your ambitions. In contrast, be with the great people who make you feel that you can become one of them."

Who knows the story of the famous tennis player André Agassi, who was ranked among the top ten players in the world? At the start of his career, he frequently lost to the inexperienced juniors. The experts advised him that it was time to retire, because he had passed the age of thirty and, according to them, would not way be able to triumph over the new youth who were full of enthusiasm, vigor, and vitality.

A friend said to him, "In order to retain your dignity and leave positives in the mind of your fans, you must retire!"

André suffered at the thought of this opinion, even if this was the logical option. At that time, he heard an inner voice saying to him, "Do not listen to these people. Everyone speaks from his own point of view. Try again, but change your style and your thoughts."

A month later, André decided to take part in international tournaments in which he achieved good results and was appointed as a human resource development expert and an expert in sports psychology. It was discovered that the secret behind André's loss was his inner thoughts, all of which were negative, revolving around weakness, age, and the inability to win.

Do not listen to those who are charging you with negative thoughts, and then there will be nothing impossible for you. You must be patient and determined to get what you want.

A Call for Hope

"There are times exactly when we feel it is the end, then we discover it is the beginning, and there are doors that we feel closed, and then we discover that it is the real entrance."

I am going to mention a story from the life of Ibrahim al-Faqi which embodies the aforementioned saying:

Al-Faqi enrolled in many correspondence courses and received an international award from America as the best student in his online class. After all this success and excellence, he lost his job again, but he did not despair and did not feel frustrated. He quickly remembered the words of his dad advising him, "If Allah shut one of the doors, son, believe that He always opens another one." If you have reached your end, believe that there is a new start. Make the best start for yourself, and do not cry about the failures of the past.

"A work without a hope leads to the loss of the work, and a hope without work leads to disappointment. Therefore, the happiness of work is found with hope, and the magnificence of hope can be found in work."

Hope is the desire to obtain a good thing, accompanied by the expectation of its happening and the complete belief that you are able to obtain it. Hope is a word that must be established in the dictionary of any human being. Indeed, without hope our life is meaningless.

Al-Faqi believes that hope is connected to work and vice versa, as they complete one another.

Ask yourself a question: is it possible for a student to succeed on hope alone?

The answer is simply: no!

"Work does not proceed except with hope, as they are two complementary forces," said Don Claus.

A Call for Work:

"When you do not know what to do, your real work starts, and when you do not know which way to go, your real journey starts."

Dr. Ibrahim al-Faqi believes that thinking is a crucial process. Goal setting is the beginning of work. Success in work needs planning—a process through which we use our available resources to achieve a specific goal within a given time period.

Planning is based on goal setting, and these goals must be standard, not extravagant.

Thus, thinking is the beginning of the process.

"What you see in your life now is only a reflection of what you have done in the past, and what you will do in the future is only a reflection of what you are doing right now."

It is as the old sayings go, "One reaps what he sows," and "The one who walks on the path, arrives."

These saying summarize the words of Al-Faqi, as those who strive in their lives will reap the fruits of their efforts.

The manager became a manager because he exerted a tremendous amount of effort in the past, and the beggar became a beggar because he did not work for his future in the past. Life is an interconnected chain. Those who work hard and faithfully will have a dazzling future. Sheikh Zayed said, "Whoever has no past, has no present or future."

Therefore, there is still time to build your present.

"**Attempt to target the focus of your life on changing your lifestyle, and start to draw the necessary energy from the stock of hidden positive abilities stored inside of you. And make the best use of your potential to become the person you want to be.**"

When we talk about potential energy, we must address James Lee Valentine, who has a thriving passion for life.

If you read James' book *Pure Power*, you will see that this book will give you strength and that his success story will positively affect you and give you strength in your life.

By harnessing your absolute power, you can organize your life in order to achieve overall success. Health, wisdom, and happiness are objectives that you can attain.

This book outlines a way to succeed in every aspect of life and will motivate you toward reaching everything that you want.

James Lee Valentine said, "Take advantage of your high power to bring out your infinite energy."

Each person has energy. Harness your energy for all that pleases Allah, and run toward the summit of success.

A Call for Optimism:

"It is possible to lose what we are afraid to lose."

There are many things that we are afraid of losing. Perhaps the first one is our parents. We do not always get to have them living with us. In addition, there are many things that can be lost from us that are beyond our control. And sometimes we lose things because of our carelessness.

Thus, you must pay a great deal of attention to what you have. Indeed, Allah has favored you above many creatures to make you in such blessings as what you have. If there are matters beyond your will, say, "Praise be to Allah," and always remember that if Allah closes one door, He will open for you another.

"Wake up happy in the morning. The sunrise shines on some people while they say, 'Good morning, O life!' while others say, 'What is this? Why did the sunrise come up again so quickly?' Beware of the negative thoughts that conquer your mind in the morning, as it is possible to program your whole day with negative feelings. Focus your attention on the pros, and start your day with a sound view of things."

What Al-Faqi is alluding to is the idea of teaching yourself optimism.

The past is very different from the future, and the disappointments of yesterday do not mean that the same will be repeated every day!

Optimism is a skill that you must learn by yourself. The problem is not what happens, but your reaction to what is happening.

The poet *Abu Qasim al-Shabi* said:
Morning shone singing for the sleeping life
The hills are dreaming under the shadow of the dangling branches
While the morning breezes are urging the dry flowers leaves to dance
The light was spreading slowly so that darkness would pass
The morning beautifully came filling the horizon with magnificence
The flowers, birds, and leaves started to thrive
The vibrant world awoke and sang to life.

We welcome the morning by saying praises of Allah for the blessings of health and wellness.

"All the flowers of tomorrow exist in the seeds of today, and all the results of tomorrow are present in today's ideas."

Ideas are what make up the essence of the human being. We plant the seeds of our future dreams today, and we reap their fruits tomorrow. So, we must run toward our dreams.

Run toward your dreams. Success is defined as passing through consecutive failures without losing your aim and persistence.

The poet Mahmoud Darwish said, "Stand on the corner of your goal and fight."

Run toward your dream and do not give in to despair. Trust in Allah. You may exhaust yourself today, but you will leave for yourself rest tomorrow. Always bear in mind that the beginning is full of work, but at the end we reap the fruits of what we sow.

A Call for a Better Life:

"When you lose hope, you lose passion. And when you lose passion, you lose sight. And when you lose insight, you lose life. We are living lost in the mirage of hope."

Dr. Al-Faqi stressed on three essential aspects upon which to build our lives: hope, passion, and insight.

Everyone should have hope in life.

What I mean by hope is the desire to fulfill something good or beautiful however negative the current circumstances are, and this only comes if you have a passion, as you must be convinced of what you are doing, not just in words, but in the work and the struggle, determination, and patience. Without passion you will lose hope. The ultimate victory is to have insight, as you should have an idea and through this idea you can build your goals with your insight and your future ambitions.

Thus, hope, passion, and insight are equal to life, and without them you are living in a mirage.

"If we have control over our emotions, we will be able to control our lives."

Let's draw for you a simple example:

When we hold the remote control through which the TV channels can be changed, we have control over this TV.

Our feelings are considered the remote control, while our lives are the TV.

Therefore, if we could control this device, the decision would be from our own selves, either to change the channel or to leave it as it is. Hence, if we could control our feelings perfectly, we would be able to control and lead our lives in a positive manner. Indeed, there is a strong relation between our feelings and our lives.

Remember, do not give your heart all of the authority over your life. Rather, think with your mind and your heart in order to attain a better quality of life.

"In fact, no human being or circumstance can force you to do something without your consent. You are the captain of your ship. You are the guard over your emotions. Your emotions are like an elevator—it goes up and down, but you are in control over it. The way you look at any situation is what causes you either happiness or unhappiness," Abraham Lincoln said.

Eleanor Roosevelt said, "No one can make you feel inferior without your consent."

The decision is in your hands, not in the hands of others.

A Call for Meditation:

"You can control yourself by controlling your thoughts. When the power of your ideas decreases, the power of the resulting feelings decreases, and you can do so by putting challenges in their natural place. Also, you can try not to make problems bigger than their actual size. Because the mind deals with the ideas that you think about, and, therefore, your emotions are emitted according to the ideas that you have resolved upon. Moreover, as long as one remains sensible, which stems from resolving upon ideas that are not exaggerated, then you will deal with your problems in a fast and easy way. However, if you exaggerate the ideas in your mind, you will lose your sensibility and there will be unwanted behaviors resulting from this, and your emotions will be more difficult to control and modify."

What Dr. Ibrahim al-Faqi means by this statement is that ideas can control and shape the self, i.e., the personality or a certain characteristic about oneself. Also, the mind works according to the nourishment of ideas that we supply it with, and our emotions may affect our thoughts. These ideas must be balanced and not exaggerated. In the case that these ideas are unbalanced, this will lead to distractions and, therefore, you will become distracted and your path in life will be unclear.

"Watch your thoughts, because they will become actions. Watch your actions, because they will become habits. Watch your habits, because they will become character. Watch your character, because it will become your destiny," said Frank Outlaw.

Thus, focus on your thoughts in order to develop your destiny.

"Ideas have more power than you could imagine. They either lead you to happiness or to misery. In either case, you are the manager of these ideas, so beware of what you think, because your thoughts will determine the reality of your current life and future life. The more positive and constructive your thoughts are, the more you lead a successful and happy life, and whenever your thoughts are negative, you are far from achieving anything positive in your life. Remember that ideas have two doors: a door to happiness and a door to misery."

You are the one who creates this door. And creating this door requires you to think with both your heart and your mind, because these ideas will determine your path now and in the future.

If you are positive, you will enjoy the door of happiness.

You will live a successful and happy life.

The sound man is the one who benefits from all the ideas he experiences during his life. Sometimes man experiences painful incidents in his life. Therefore, be strong, as the strong one is the one who holds a degree of influence over the ideas surrounding him in life. As a result, you must be sane, strong, and positive.

"Your eyes are a mere reflection of your inner thoughts."

What may seem beautiful to you may not look beautiful to someone else, because we don't see with our eyes alone but also with our thoughts which stem from our emotions, feelings, and previous programming.

For instance, you see a woman who married an ugly-looking man. In your perspective, she is a gorgeous woman.

Some of us might say, "How is it possible for that woman to marry that man?!"

The answer is simply that they are not seeing one another through your eyes! Each of us is definitely influenced by our thoughts when we see things. Indeed, the thoughts of mankind are varied.

Thus, the eyes reflect the way you think and your thoughts.

"Ideas become things. If you imagine them in your mind, you are on your way to carrying them in your hand," said Bob Proctor.

A Call for Smiling:

**"Always keep your attractive smile beaming on your face.
Even if you do not feel like you want to smile, pretend to smile, because the subconscious mind is incapable of distinguishing between the real and the fake. Based on this rule, it is better to choose to smile constantly."**

Dr. Al-Faqi has a similar saying to this one, "If you see someone you love, smile so that he can feel your love. And if you see your enemy, smile so that he will feel your strength. If you see someone who has left you, smile so that he will feel remorse. If you see someone who you don't know, smile so that you will gain rewards."

Smiling shows self-confidence and positivity. In addition, it is the language that does not require translation.

Pay attention to this Thai wisdom, "The smile is the easiest way to get to the heart of others."

"If you are not happy internally, you will not be happy on the outside. If you are not as happy as you want to be now, you will not be happy when you get what you want. Therefore, if you are not happy with your life now, you will not be happy with any life."

Smile. Try to make yourself smile, and always be optimistic. It is an equation. If you are sad internally, you will be sad on the outside. If you invite sadness to become your companion, sadness will be happy to be with you. Therefore, do not despair despite how difficult your situation is! Plant seeds of optimism, and attempt to exert efforts to develop your smile.

Always remember that sadness is only a waste of your precious time. Therefore, renew the hope in your heart, and rush quickly toward your goals. Be happy whatever the circumstances are.

Nothing is more beautiful than smiling to the people. Smiling to others is a charity, and it plants the seeds of love inside hearts.

Smile, all of you! We believe in the religion of happiness, as it is mentioned by our Prophet, peace and blessings be upon him, that the one who smiles upon meeting his brother, a good deed is recorded for him.

A Call for Doing Good Deeds:

"Be the one who initiates the greetings of peace to others. Our great Prophet, peace and blessings be upon him, said in his prophetic hadith, 'The better of the two is the one who says the greeting of peace first.'[1] Hence, do not wait for anyone to give you his hand; be the one to initiate it."

The first thing that must be offered in human social interaction is the feeling of safety, comfort, and stability. There is no value of human life when these elements are unavailable.

These elements originate from peace and they mean praying for the person you love and asking for safety and trying to coexist. Peace means being the first to greet people and to forgive others and take the initiative in doing so. Peace has other noble meanings, the most prominent of them being forgiveness, love, intimacy, closeness, and humility.

Indeed, the one who acquires peace is the one who has acquired Allah's love and support.

Be an initiator of peace for the sake of earning Allah's love and also for the sake of humanity.

---

[1] Yahya related to me from Malik from Ibn Shihab from Ata ibn Yazid al-Laythi from Abu Ayyub al-Ansari that the Messenger of Allah, may Allah bless him and grant him peace, said, "It is not halal for a Muslim to shun his brother for more than three nights, that is they meet, and this one turns away and that one turns away. The better of the two is the one who says the greeting first."

A Call for Learning:

"Be an attentive ear. Bear in mind that this is not an easy matter at all, as it might take you some time until you adapt to this. Thus, start from now. Do not interrupt anyone during his stream of speech, and you must show interest. Be always an attentive ear."

It's easy to be a hearer, but it's difficult to be an attentive listener. There is a remarkable difference between hearing and attentive listening. Hearing is the process of receiving a message through the ear, whereas attentive listening means that you should use the ears, organs, senses, the heart, and the mind to understand the meaning intensively. For this reason, Dr. Al-Faqi said, "It is not an easy matter at all."

Adapt yourself to be an attentive listener, and avoid interrupting one when he speaks. Also, pay close attention to be able to learn, and put all of your concentration on listening attentively.

Al-Hassan al-Basri said, "If you are given the chance to sit with the scholars, take care to listen more than to try to talk. Concern yourself with developing the best listening skills as well as the skills of remaining silent and not interrupting someone else's speech."

"The face is the mirror of the mind and eyes. Without speaking, it tells the secrets of the heart."

There is a language of the face and a language of the eyes, as the face reflects what the mind thinks, and the eyes reveal what the heart is hiding, as well as showing if a person is lying.

A lie detector has the ability to detect the liar, and it may be wrong if the person is trained in deception, but in the case of relying on facial expression, in addition to the movement of the eyes, it is impossible for a person to lie and fool the psychologists or the specialists and scholars who are concerned with such matters. In fact, there are involuntary indicators that occur in the case of lying. Experts are able to detect the liar by the distance between the lips and ears, the distance between the eyes and the ears, facial expressions, and the color of the cheeks. Did you know that in the case of lying there are 14 changes that occur in the face?

There are hints in the eyes of the visual, auditory, and sensory person:

Visual person: The eyes are turned up, then to the left. This movement is for remembering information.

Visual Imagination: The two eyes turn up, and then to the right. This movement indicates a hidden response, so we have to imagine it.

Non-centered Remembering: The eyes are stable and not moving, and the sight is directed ahead toward you.

Know that your facial features and your eyes are able to show what is in your heart.

"Communication is like a flash; no matter how dark the night is; it always lights up the road."

Communication: It is the light through which you will open new doors, and the process of correspondence, through which people share information and experiences and convey messages amongst themselves.

Through information, sharing of opinions, and discussion, we will reach new horizons, and our perceptions will expand.

"Learn to adapt with all kinds of people, and keep yourself in constant contact until the uneven parts of your mind smoothen, and that's something you can't do if you're isolated," said Dale Carnegie.

A Call for Implanting the Values of Positivity:

"From today, begin to treat others in the way that you would like them to treat you.

From today, smile at others in the way that you would like them to smile at you.

From today, praise others in the way that you would like for them to praise you.

From today, listen to others in the way that you would like them to listen to you.

From today, help others in the way that you would like them to help you.

That way, you are going to reach the highest summit of success, and you are going to be on your way to unlimited happiness."

Be the role model and the one who races toward all positivity. Sow good, and you are going to reap good. Don't forget to smile, so that people can imitate you when they see you doing so. Do not contradict yourself in your words and actions.

Allah the Almighty says in His Holy Qur'an: (O you who have believed, why do you say what you do not do? Great is hatred in the sight of Allah that you say what you do not do.[2])

This double personality suffers from schizophrenia—do not say what you do not do! Because this behavior is not pleasing to Allah.

---

[2] Surah As-Saf: [61: (4,5)]

Moreover, it is bothersome to your conscience. If you follow this road, you will live in delusion, depression, and illness—schizophrenia. In the end, you will lose success, and happiness will lose its way to you.

"Be yourself!

Be positive. Think about what you want, not what you do not want. Take initiative. Think about what you have drawn out and planned for.

Be yourself, understanding the essence of life, envisioning crossing into the future safely.

Be yourself. Be assured that you will obtain guidance that will affirm your future success.

Don't imitate any other, as he will not think about what you desire, and even if he did, it would be about what he wants. Be sure that the other will not be more initiative and responsive to your needs than your own self! The other will not draw out your future and plan your set of goals. Undoubtedly, he is not going to understand your life the same way that you understand it. The other who you imitate does not care for helping you in your affairs. But when you settle it on your own, there will be rest for your heart, not his."

A Call from Dr. Al-Faqi to Not Change the Essence of the Self:

The one who disrespects his own soul through the imitation of others is the one who burns his soul. The one who disrespects his own soul will also be disrespected by others. Therefore, secure for yourself the values of positivity, initiative, understanding, and rest, so that you can live as you desire. Leave others to live as they please, because you are the captain of your own ship. You are going to create your future by your own hands and not by theirs. Consequently, focus your interest on your affairs and do not neglect them. Always be a runner toward your self-development and the advancement of your future. Gandhi said, "Be the change that you wish to see in the world."

"Remember that winter is the beginning of the summer, darkness is the beginning of light, pressure is the beginning of rest, and failure is the beginning of success."

All of us will suffer. We will all taste bitterness, as this is the theme of life. If it were not for our sins, we would not have learned. Know that we learn throughout life each day, which adds new value.

Jean Valgan suffered from failure and difficulty in his life, because he was a negative person, and this is the story of Victor Hugo mentioned in his novel, *Les Miserables*.

In Brief:

Jean Valgan was a burglar and a criminal, and his life was grim. He faced much contempt from the people of his village, but because of the action of one person his life changed from darkness to light. Then, he became a mayor and gained much love from the people. Afterwards, he changed his name so that people would not discover his true identity. He completely changed himself for the better.

It is a long story and the incidents were exciting. But someone who is a thief turns into someone who serves people as much as he can. In fact, He began to do the good everywhere. This is the story of Jean. He realized that his past was dark and he worked on changing the path of his life.

Know that when you drive your car, maybe one time you may take a wrong route away from your destination. Then, you will be able to change your path, and this is a lesson for you to avoid making mistakes next time.

"Success does not consist in never making mistakes but in never making the same one a second time," said George Bernard Shaw.

"Address people by name, I think our names are the most beautiful thing our ears hear."

The name of man is the thing that remains with the human being since birth and even after his death. This name remains with him, it is natural that the person loves his name, because the parents are those who chose this name for us, how do we not love it?!

How beautiful when people call us by our names! In calling us with our names, all feelings of affection and love open, and from the Sunnah, if it is said to someone: Who are you? He should call/introduce himself under his name, and it is not preferred to say (I) or calling someone with his/her offensive nickname.

Allah the Almighty said in Surah Al-Hujurat: (and do not call each other by [offensive] nicknames)

Always remember that your morals make your name more shining.

"Remember that a person's name is to that person the sweetest and most important sound in any language," said Dale Carnegie.

A Call for Challenging:

"If you looked closely around you, you will figure out that the true challenge in life is to change yourself to better and be the person you want to be. Moreover, you will find that you should exploit all of your inner possibilities and live a happy life. A Life that is free from impotence, restrictions and negative emotions. Referring that, when you focus your attention on blaming others, you waste your energies and abilities and waste your time. Instead, try to focus on changing your lifestyle and start drawing the necessary energy from the stock of hidden positive abilities stored inside you. In addition, take advantage of your potential to become the human being who you wished to be."

There is no better than to change yourself for the better as life is renewed every day. Every day must be better than yesterday, and you must make the best use of your energies. Undoubtedly, everyone on this planet has an advantage and able to contribute to the development of himself/herself and the development of his/her society. We all dream and all of us hope. Thus, know that if you wish something, you will be able to reach it, but enough that you thought about this thing; because you are capable, and you did not think in vain.

Focus on this goal, and you will reach the goal of your thinking and your wish, provided that you erase from your heart and your mind the word *miraculous* or *impossible*, and remember that: There is neither despair with life, nor life with despair.

"In the science of metaphysics, scholars always emphasize that the mind, like a magnet, when its owner feels that he/she achieves his/her goals, even by imagining, this will attract people, coincidences, and mechanisms that will help him/her to achieve this goal."

For Instance:

When I was in the university, I imagined and worked my best for the degree of excellence; my mind indirectly was programmed to this goal, and with the passage of days, conditions, attitudes, and appropriate mechanisms, Allah the Almighty achieved this goal for me. Praise be to Allah, at the end, I graduated with the highest degree of honor!

In his book *Alchemist*, Paulo Coelho said: "If you desire to achieve or obtain something, the whole world will work on obeying you to achieve your desire."

"Failures attack those who sit in their place waiting for success to hit their doors."

What a beauty when you challenge yourself while you are stepping forward to the best.

The poet *Abu al-Qasim al-Shabi* said:
Whoever gives up afraid of climbing the mountain
He might not get the blessings of the running fountain.

It is beautiful that you see yourself a white bird spreading peace among the humanity. It is also beautiful that you became like a flower filling the life with fragrance and love. But the most beautiful thing is when you exploit your energy for doing the good and achieving your goal. Indeed, this goal must be a noble one.

Know that every human being has strong potential energy, and this energy has no limits, so do not let it go in vain, and exploit it to live a better life.

Be aware that your abilities are beyond the limits. Then, accept your inner self, no matter how people mock you, and always say to yourself: You are the best creature made by the hand of Allah. There is an English saying that says: "What does not kill you makes you stronger."

"There are times when we feel that it is the end. Whilst, we figure out that it is just the start. In addition, there are doors we think it is closed tightly. Then, we figure out that it is the right entrance and beginning."

If you think about changing the destiny of your life, you have to change your way of realization.

In this position, we can feel the magnificence of Allah's saying in Surah Ar-Ra'ad: *(Indeed, Allah will not change the condition of a people until they change what is in themselves.)*

Human being is the cause of creating the idea, he/she is the determiner of his fate. Therefore, human being should avoid putting himself as a prey for the negative concentration on certain idea. He/she must not blame the others on irrevocability. Instead, he has to start with himself.

Sheikh Sha'rawi, may Allah be pleased with him, said in his book *Khawater*: "When movement meets up with sight, herein comes the happiness."

A Call for Reaching the Goal:

"It does not reduce from the hardness of marble its being shiny and polished."

A person who is well-trained and has self-esteem cannot be held back by anyone. Always remember that a conscious, aware, sensible, and capable human being is like gold, no matter how dust spreads over it. Over time, it will remain a precious commodity.

You are the one who shapes his/her personality. You are the person who imposes his/her character. Therefore, be gold so you will not get rust or be affected by the babbling of the others.

There is a wisdom that says: The strong person is who does not pay even a little attention for the words of people but in fact he steps firmly toward his goal.

"The most flexible person can control his sensations. Moreover, he is capable of achieving his goals more than the person who has no flexibility; this is because the flexible person if he thought about a method that could not help him to reach his goal, he rethinks again about a different method that gives him the required results. Thus, he can achieve his goals.

The mechanism to live a better life is: balance, discipline, determination on achieving the goals, access to sight, flexibility in style, then patience, and trust in Allah the Almighty."

Flexibility means: the ability to form in different shapes, while flexibility according to mankind means: the ability to control and adapt, so that the human is smooth.

The flexible human being: He is the man who is capable of adapting to the environment with the resources available to him and capable of achieving his goals.

Through flexibility, human being can lead a better life; As the elements of achieving success are being provided, which are: balance – discipline – persistence on reaching the goal – sight – flexibility in style. Eventually, patience and trust in Allah, the Exalted and Glorified in the heavens.

Always remember that any work requires your efforts and a complete trust in Allah.

You cannot be committed to a certain work and a goal that you desire to achieve without the required flexibility, as flexibility is a strength; because the person who has this trait, he/she can have perfect control on his nerves. Consequently, he/she reaches his/her goals.

"The human being who thinks in a sound way, he will know exactly what goals is he searching. Moreover, he will know the end of these goals. When he reaches what he opts for, he will see from there what is the farthest."

Watch your thoughts carefully, as they are the creator of your coming future. Get rid of the bad ones and fight every idea that attempts to get you down or makes your way of thinking looks inferior or restrict your abilities.

Socrates said: "With the intellect, man can plant his world of roses or thorns."

Therefore, human being should think in a sound way; so that he can reap the great noble goals.

There are those who pass through life struggling, getting tired, and sweating. But at the end, they do not reap anything; because they neglected the value of thinking and planning. Moreover, they did not create for themselves a detailed program answering this question: what do I want? And how can I do what I want?

The person who does not think, he might succeed, but the difficulties that faces him are a lot and harder than the person who has an integral plan and obvious goals. It is not intelligence and tact to replace what is good with what is bad.

When you reach your goals, you have to forget that there is a second place. Your eyes must be focused on the top first position. As President Kennedy said, "Once you are satisfied with the second place, you will not reach further than what you achieved."

"Be careful that your goals become just wishful thinking, or desires… as this is the goods of the poor."

Achieve your goals, work hard to achieve them, and try to implant within you strong and brilliant goals; with your efforts you will achieve your goals.

There are a lot of people who live in the circle of wishes, not working a little to make their dreams a reality.

What is the value of the goal which is not pushed by a desire?

The strong desire is the oxygen which is breathed by the goals so that it can be embodied in the reality.

Goals without a strong desire are just lazy dead goals lacking the spirit. Therefore, your desire to achieve your dream must be a burning, flowing, rushing toward the summit one. Moreover, it must not be stoppable, even by you.

"I'm determined to reach my goal. Either I'll succeed or I'll succeed," said Dale Carnegie.

Always make sure that your goal is stemmed from your inner values and principles, and that it revolves around them, never leaving them.

All you have to do is to commence from now, and before any other time, put your hopes and dreams on paper. Face your dream face to face, and know it closely. You should not be fooled by delaying the work of today till tomorrow, but say, "Tomorrow, I will be, the decision is mine, the dream is mine." And always, fate is biased toward the serious and sincere people.

A Call for Approaching Allah:

"The quickest way to have enemies is to complain continuously to your friends."

I will summarize this saying depending on the words of the Prophet, peace and blessings be upon him, "Let him speak good or be silent."

The more you complain to the people specially the friends and the more you speak with them negatively, the more negativity chase you. Sometimes, we are not aware of what we are saying specially in the state of sadness, tension, and anger. Watch out from going to your friends several times to vent your anger and complain. Do not give them the complete trust; because we are living in an era where trust does not exist anymore. It is not necessary to say everything and know that you have the time and right to complain and seek Allah's relief. Indeed, He is the only One who can hear you at any time and at any place. He is the One who is going to rescue you from your ordeal not your friends.

Mentioning Noah, the Prophet peace and blessing be upon him, when the harm of his people reached an unbearable end and when they seized and threatened him, they were taking any one followed him and afflicting him till he changed his religion, "So he invoked his Lord, 'Indeed, I am overpowered, so help.'" [Surah Al-Qamar: (54:10)]

Allah provided Noah with his victory, and he punished the disbelievers with the great flood. Indeed, Noah and his followers became the triumphant ones.

"Do not tear yourself down on what happens with you in this life, we are created herein to be examined and inflicted; so that Allah sees if we are going to be patients? Therefore, feel relief and do not get sad. Believe that the relief is soon. Make sure that when the sky gets darker and cloudy, it means that soon the rains are going to pour down."

In this life, there is the happy, and there is the miserable. But whatever your moment is, do not stop saying: *Alhamdulilah* (Praise be to Allah) every now and then, in every time and place. You do not know what will happen to you after then?!

Remember that if Allah shuts one door, He is able to open another one.

It is mentioned that our prophet Ayyub (Job), peace and blessing be upon him, caught a contagious disease which is called Leprosy. It is rendered one of the most dangerous diseases as the skin gets eroded and spoiled. Moreover, the disease remained attacking him for 18 years!

In that period of time, all people left him except his faithful wife. His tongue did not stop mentioning Allah while his heart was satisfied and his body was patient. He was like a steadfast mountain! Throughout his illness, he was thanking Allah and calling Him per day and night. Allah said in Surah Al-Anbya: (So We responded to him and removed what afflicted him of adversity. And We gave him [back] his family and the like thereof with them as mercy from Us and a reminder for the worshippers [of Allah].) [21:84]

Ayyub, peace and blessing be upon him, after a while recovered from this dangerous disease.

Bear always in your mind that patience is the key for relief.

"Materialistic life in which we are living, the strong competition that we see around us, and the rapid change made most of the people lose the life in the stream of challenges. Moreover, this situation made them get away

from Allah the Almighty either the person realizes that or not."

Do you know someone whose life is a series of problems, hardships, and difficulties? Adding that, if he tries to get out of a problem, he enters another one?

If your answer is yes, do you know the main cause in that?

All the problem lies in his distancing oneself from Allah, the Exalted and Glorified in the heavens. Undoubtedly, the true believer trusts Allah, fears, and praises Him in both happy and hard moments. In addition, he does not stop getting closer to Allah. Whereas the person who distances himself from Allah, the life becomes his all interest and it becomes miserable full of negativities.

Let's mention for you a story in brief:

There was a landlord who owned millions of dollars. His life was revolving around one thing that is called money. He was distancing himself from the high spiritual matters. In addition, his speaking dictionary was only about investments, real estates, and selling. Unfortunately, he did not mention the grace of Allah upon him even for one time. The years passed away and he was hit by a disease out of a huge project in which he participated with all of his money. Sadly, he lost all of his fortune so that he could not bear hearing the bad news and he was paralyzed as a result of the shock.

His friend told him that without a doubt Allah, the Exalted and Glorified in the heavens, loves you, therefore, he placed you in this challenge to open for you another door so you can approach Him, the Almighty.

In that time, he cried intensively. Then, he said, "When I get out of here, I will be a new person and I will approach Allah, the Exalted and Glorified in the heavens."

His friend asked him, "Do you guarantee that you can get out of here in full recovery?"

He replied in a sad tone, "No!"

His friend said, "So, do not wait till you get out of here. Start from Fatiha now and praise Allah the Almighty. Let's read Surah Al-Fatiha."

Afterwards, he said, "I have not felt this tranquility since a long period of time."

His friend commented on his words, "This is the sensation that you feel with Allah, the Exalted and Glorified in the heavens."

As Allah said, (And whoever turns away from My remembrance – indeed, he will have a depressed life, and We will gather him on the Day of Resurrection blind.3)

---

³ Surah Taha: [20:124]

A Call for Tolerance:

"Forgive your enemies, but never forget their names."[4]

The Prophet, peace and blessings be upon him, taught us to react to the offence by forgiving. Most of us remember the event of the conquest of Mecca, when he said to the people of Quraysh when they came to see what will he do with them after triumphing upon them, "No blame will there be upon you today. Go, we will forgive you."

Nothing is more beautiful than forgiving, tolerating, and avoiding the revenge when you are capable!

Forgive, get away from your enemies but do not take revenge. Tolerate, but do not forget their names; therefore, you can ignore them in the future and do not think that tolerance is an offense to you. But it is the highest stages of the maturity of human being. Moreover, your knowing to these persons is a benefit; because you learn from life the mechanism of selecting the friends. Thanks all my friends!

"Tolerance is a moral which can be learnt easily, but its application is hard."

There are those who say that tolerance is weak. When there is a quarrel between two people about a particular subject, you will see everyone fleeing from tolerance, thinking that he will become the weaker party!

---

[4] John F. Kennedy

Unfortunately, the concept of tolerance in society has become an insult and weakness; it is a rule for the other side to win when we apologize!

Did you know that tolerance brings you positive thinking. Whereas, intolerance brings you negative feelings and sensations?! We do not have time in this world of sadness, distress, and anger of a certain person, or a specific position.

And remember that when forgiving, you will receive a reward from Allah, and your thinking will become positive. If Allah, the Lord of the people, can forgive and tolerate, why do not we forgive while we are the slaves?! If our Prophet and Messenger, Mohammed, who is the most honorable and role model of all creation, forgives, why do not we forgive?!

If Allah is oft-forgiving and most Merciful, why do not we forgive or tolerate the mistakes of others?!

Anas (RA) narrated that Allah's Messenger (ﷺ) said:

"All the sons of Adam are sinners, but the best of sinners are those who repent often." Related by Al-Tirmidhi and Ibn Majah with a strong chain of narrators.

Tolerate, because you may fall in mistakes one day.

Gandhi said: "When you forgive, you in no way change the past – but you sure do change the future."

A Call for the Continuity of Success:

"If people attacked you and you are right or you are being criticized, rejoice, they say you are successful and influential, the dead dog does not kick or throw except the fruitful trees."

If people around you are talking about you or standing in front of you, labeling you with traits that are not of your character, or trying to distort your image, or talk negatively, know that in this way, they tell you that you are indirectly successful, and remember that the dog only kicks the fruit tree to get it.

What more dogs in this age!

Let them say what they want, they did not find in the gold any flaw, they said, "Its shining hurts the eyes."

Finally, no one challenges your reputation unless he/she wishes to be like you and he could not.

A Call for Exploiting the Time:

"Every day when the sun shines, it calls upon us... I am a new day and on your work is a witness, so take advantage of me, I will not return till the Day of Resurrection, and take advantage of every moment in your life."

Time is the most precious possession we have in this life. We do our best to lose and kill its value. We stay not aware of its value and we kill ourselves as time is the true life as what is said.

There is a superstition spread among people which is "I do not have time." Create a saying for yourself: "One day I will have enough time to achieve what is late."

Getting free from the superstition of not having the enough time is the first step from which you rocket up toward an organized life.

Al-Hassan Al-Basri said: "Oh son of Adam, you are a mere amount of days. If your day is gone, your life will be gone."

The sane person makes the best use of his time in an organized way. Moreover, he does not let the little matters distract him and control his life.

Time is the most precious thing you own and the greatest to be invested on. Undoubtedly, it is your life, present and future. In addition, it is your start and end. Therefore, deal with your time seriously and decisively.

A Call for Having Patience:

"If you are not patient enough, this will lead to the demolition of your dreams."

Lack of patience is one of the causes that leads to failure; because before you reach the success station, you would have gone through obstacles, barriers, and temporary challenges. Hence, if you do not have patience, you will not be able to exceed these challenges. Consequently, you are going to give up on achieving your dreams.

Allah the Almighty said in Surah Al-Baqarah, (Give good tidings to the patient.)

"Patience is the best remedy for every trouble," said Plautus.

Adhere to patience and enthusiasm; perhaps there are few steps on reaching your success.

"Many of life's failures are people who did not realize how close they were to success when they gave up," said Thomas A. Edison.

Be patient, achieve your dreams, be the person who takes the opportunity, and do not be the person who creates the problem of every opportunity.

Norman Vincent mentioned in his book *The Power of Positive Thinking*, "Don't be discouraged. It's often the last key in the bunch that opens the lock."

Dr. Ibrahim Al-Faqi's Death

Dr. Ibrahim al-Faqi, the Egyptian expert in the science of Human Resource Development and Linguistic Programming, and the chairman of the Canadian Institute for Language Programming, faced his end in a gigantic fire in the apartment where he lived on Friday, February 10th, 2012.

The fire broke out on the third floor of Dr. Ibrahim al-Faqi Psychiatric Center, located on Makram Ebeid Street, Nasr City, and spread to the rest of the properties owned by al-Faqi where he lived. The fire led to the death of Dr. al-Faqi at the age of 62, and his sister Fuqiya Mohammed al-Faqi at the age of 72, and the baby sitter who was living with them, according to the Egyptian mass media.

The Civil Defense Forces were able to control the fire, and the three dead bodies were taken to the hospital. The prosecution of the city of Nasr investigated the cause of the fire. Dr. Ibrahim's nephew, whose mom was killed in the fire, pointed out that there were a large number of heaters in the house. This may be the cause of the fire, while some media indicated that a small fire broke out in an internal wooden staircase, then spread to the rest of the building.

Abu Hurairah (May Allah be pleased with him) reported:

The Messenger of Allah (ﷺ) said, "When a man dies, his deeds come to an end except for three things: Sadaqah Jariyah (ceaseless charity); a knowledge which is beneficial, or a virtuous descendant who prays for him (for the deceased)."

Narrated by **[Muslim]**

No one can deny how much knowledge we are benefited from you, Dr. al-Faqi, and we are not forgetting you in our prayers...

(May Allah be pleased with you Dr. al-Faqi and may He pour his mercy upon you).

Epilogue

Talking about Ibrahim al-Faqi is not an easy matter. In fact, one book is not enough to show his true position. He is the one who enlightened the path for millions of people, he is the candle of hope for any human being in a dark ordeal. Moreover, we have learned from him so much and are still learning and learning as his life is various experiments. In addition, his experiences are rendered moral lessons.

His words and sayings are as bright as the stars shining in the sky. His style is characterized with a distinctive charismatic shape. Indeed, no one can occupy his position except one person: Dr. Ibrahim al-Faqi himself.

Dr. Ibrahim al-Faqi taught us to think positively, act positively, and learn how to improve our lives to reach a better life. He taught us to always expect the best to happen.

The greatest thing I can gift you in this Epilogue are the words that were deduced from the prophet, peace and blessings be upon him when he said, "Optimistic goodness shall find."

Finally, live every moment as if it is the last one in your life, live with hope, with struggle, with following of the morals of the prophet, peace and blessings be upon him, the faithful companions, and the righteous worshipers. Appreciate the value of life and be unique.

Ibrahim Al-Faqi in Lines

- Founder and Chairman of the Ibrahim Al Faqi International Group of Companies.
- Founder and Chairman of the Canadian Teaching Center for Hypnosis (CTCH), and the Canadian Teaching Center of Human Development (CTCHD), and the Canadian Center for Neuro-Linguistic Programming. (CTCNLP)
- Founder and Chairman of CUBES (CIS)
- Doctor of Metaphysics from the University of Metaphysics, Los Angeles, United States.
- Dr. Ibrahim al-Faqi is the author of Neuro Conditioning Dynamics – NCD.
- Founder of Power Human Energy – PHE.
- Certified trainer in NLP, from the American Foundation for Neuro-Linguistic Programming.
- Certified trainer for Hypnotherapy from the American Institute of Hypnosis.
- Certified trainer for Time Line Therapy
- A certified memory trainer from the American Institute of Memory in New York.
- Certified trainer for Human Development from the Government of Quebec, Canada, for companies and institutions.
- Reiki coach from The Reiki Training Center of Canada, and from the Global Reiki Association
- Holds the first honorary degree in human behavior from the American Hotels Corporation.
- Holds first honor degree in management, sales, and marketing from the American Hotels Corporation.

- Has 23 diplomas, and three of the highest specializations in psychology, management, sales, marketing, and human development.
- Served as general manager for several five-star hotels in Montreal – Canada.
- Has several books, translated into three languages: (English, French, and Arabic), and has achieved sales of more than one million copies in the world.
- Trained more than 700,000 people in his lectures around the world. He lectured and trained in three languages: English, French, and Arabic.
- Egypt's former champion in table tennis and represented Egypt in the World Championship in West Germany, in 1969.
- Lived in Montreal, Canada, with his wife Amal and their twin daughters Nancy and Nermin, then moved to Egypt.
- This great man died on February 10th, 2012.

A Message from a Friend

From today…

Pay close attention to your thoughts before they turn to an unchangeable focus point,

Note your concentration before it turns into a sensation,

Watch your feeling before it turns into a behavior,

Note your behavior before it turns into results,

Note your results before they determine your destiny.

You are not the title you gave to yourself,

Or the title given to you by the others,

You are not depression, anxiety, or frustration,

Or tension or failure.

You are not your age, your weight, your shape, your size, or your color. You are not the past, neither the present nor the future.

You are the best creature created by Allah the Almighty. If any human being has achieved anything in this world, you can also achieve it, and even surpass it, if Allah wills.

Always remember that:
Night is the beginning of the day,
Winter is the beginning of the summer,
Pain is the beginning of rest,
The challenges are the beginning of good,
Optimism is the beginning of self-strength.
Therefore…
Live every moment as if it is the last moment of your life…
Live with your love to Allah, the Almighty…
Live by imitating the ethics of the Prophet peace and blessings be upon him…
Live with hope, live with struggle, live with patience…
Live with love, appreciate the value of life…
And be unique…

Will of Love

With patience and trust in Allah you can achieve your goals. Accept yourself completely. Whatever challenges and circumstances you face, you are not your behavior, challenges, and sensations. All these are activities and what happens is a reaction toward them…

Whatever people think and feel, accept yourself…

Make yourself an inner self-image while you are achieving your goals sanely. Be confident in yourself and your unlimited abilities, learn the strategies that will help you use your potentialities and strengthen your belief. Moreover, it strengthens your thoughts and goals until you have the feeling that you deserve to achieve your goals as you did your best and struggled. Therefore, turn all your energy to Allah the Almighty, love him, and know his position and power, seek his help, trust him, and sincerely work hard and be professional on it. Eventually, you will be happy in this life and hereafter.

The Most Remarkable Words
Said About Dr. Ibrahim Al-Faqi

"Dr. al-Faqi is considered a gift from Allah to help all humanity," said Karim Suleiman – Director of Finance, Algerian Islamic Scouts, Algeria

"A summit in knowledge, magnificence and creativity. Moreover, he is more knowledgeable than what we imagined as his sacrifice in spreading the knowledge turned into great generosity," said Ghoneim Abdulrahman Nayef Abdul Rahman Al Hajri – External Mass Media Sector, Kuwait

"Dr. Ibrahim al-Faqi is a wonderful lecturer, believes in what he says, reaches to our minds and hearts directly," said Iman Sabri Othman – Director of Al Waha Language School, Mokattam, Cairo, Egypt

"Dr. Ibrahim al-Faqi is a great scientist, and humble professor, words are incapable to show how appreciation we carry for him," said Hassan Ali Kayal – Saudi Airlines, Jeddah, Kingdom of Saudi Arabia

"Dr. Ibrahim al-Faqi is a great intellectual, psychological, moral, and spiritual energy that is characterized by the beauty of presentation. Moreover, his spirit is easy going one," said Nada Ali Abdullah Ghuloom – Bahrain United Kingdom

"Dr. Al-Faqi is a global lecturer, the words are not enough to describe his presence," said Ahmed Ali – Engineer, Amsterdam, The Netherlands

"He is a turning point in the life of every human being who wishes to be distinguished and Dr. Ibrahim al-Faqi has a strong presence, unique style. Moreover, he is an affectionate father," said Kamal Mohammed Omara – Head of Human Resources and Administrative Affairs, Dubai, The United Arab Emirates

"Dr. Al-Faqi is one of the most powerful lecturers in the world, Allah gave him power to achieve what he satisfies," said Hamad bin Hamoud bin Suleiman Al-Fafri – Head of Activities, Sultan Qaboos University, Muscat, Sultanate of Oman

"Dr. al-Faqi gave me twenty years' experience in one lecturer. Undoubtedly, he is a wonderful lecturer, enters the heart and mind," said Ribwar Mohamed Amin Rashid – imam and preacher, and a master student in origins of religion, Iraq

"I did not expect this amount of information and skills I had mastered, and Dr. Ibrahim Al-Faqi is resourceful, and very professional more than you can ever imagine," said Mohammed Ahmed al- 'Atn – Engineer, Nile Company for rubber and plastic, Alexandria, Egypt

"Dr. Ibrahim Al-Faqi is a gift from Allah, the Exalted and Glorified in the heavens," said Sami Ghattas – Doctor, Tunisia

"In my opinion, Dr. Ibrahim al-Faqi is considered one of the best global lecturers," said Bernadette Descartes – Broadcaster, CBL, Louisiana, United States of America

"He is more than wonderful, unrivaled skill in the art of presentation," said Dr. Clement Johnson – Doctor, Texas, United States of America

"He is fun and resourceful, he reaches to the heart of the listener in a quick sharp way that I did not see before," said Christian McDonald – Bristol Myers, Montreal, Canada

"Dr. Ibrahim al-Faqi taught me the art of life, and lit my way to happiness," said Michelle Goian – Editor in Actuality Newspaper, Montreal, Canada

"Dr. Ibrahim Al-Faqi's seminars are a lifetime experience and the opportunity to attend must be available for each individual," said Rose Sulazo – Montreal, Canada

"Dr. Ibrahim Al-Faqi lit me the way to a new quest," said Suzette Gordo – Canadian Airlines, Canada

"He is Unique, and is considered one of the most powerful global lecturers," said France Martel – TV presenter Quebec, CPM channel, Canada

"He is one of the few lecturers in the world who have such capabilities and skills, and have benefited me more than I expected," said Yousef Ahmed Jibril – Planning and Development Authority, Dubai

"Dr. Ibrahim Al-Faqi is considered one of the most powerful modern lecturers," said Molhem Mohammed Hussein – National Marketing Foundation, Saudi Arabia

"He enlightened in our hearts the love and attachment to his personality, and this is a rare hard equation," said Odette Iskandar – Chairman of the Board of Directors of Egypt and the Middle East, Egypt

"He is excellent, and distinctive. Moreover, his style is interesting, and his lecture touched my heart and my sense, and changed the flow of my thinking in life," said Azza Farhat – Human Resources Manager, Egypt

"Dr. Ibrahim Al-Faqi plays special music, fills the inner worlds with energy; it pushes the others towards the real movie of life, charged with dynamic and raging desire to excellence," said Mona Abdul Jalil – Journalist, Kuwait

"He is very excellent, I did not expect him to be in such humble character, and caring attitude towards the trainees," said Abdullah Harith Al Rumaithi – Head of Music Department, Radio and Television of Dubai, United Arab Emirates

"Dr. Ibrahim Al-Faqi is a pride to the Arab and Islamic Nation," said Haytham Abdul Ghani – Deputy General Manager, Saudi Import & Export Company of paper, United Kingdom of Saudi Arabia

"He is imaginative, creative, dynamic personality. I did not expect to meet someone like him in our Arab world," said Faisal Mishary Al – Mu'ammar, National Health Services Company, Saudi Arabia

"Dr. Ibrahim Al-Faqi is one of the leading specialists in human development in the world," said Darren Montgomery – TV Louisiana, United States of America

"I have not seen anyone in his unlimited work," said Ilan Blunes – Canada TV

"Dr. Ibrahim El-Faqi is one of the best lecturers in the era," said Alain LaRouche – Montreal TV, Canada

"A self-indulgent personality, resourceful till the utmost limits, and able to deliver the information easily," said Brad Mayzer – London, England

"Dr. Ibrahim Al-Faqi's lectures were one of the best and most powerful lectures. Moreover, it caught the admiration and appreciation of all people," said Mahasin El Bakry – Hilton Worldwide Company.

"He is unlimited power and energy, and unrivaled ingenuity in the art of appreciation," said Mushiera – Al-Barad'ei, Director of Human Resources, American University, Cairo

"He is a great energy, wonderful, talented, tremendous encyclopedia of information. We are proud of him as the top Arab Muslim in his field," said Zahraa Abdul Hamid Al-issa – Abdul Hameed Al-issa Foundation, Kuwait

"Dr. Ibrahim Al-Faqi is considered a treasure for the Arab and the Islamic nation," said Eid Falah Al-Ghasham – Jaber Al-Ali association, Kuwait

"The best of whom I ever seen," said Saeed Abdullah Al-Mazloum – Quality Control Manager, Dubai Police

Sources and References

- Al-Arabiya.net (the death of al-Faqi's news) Http://www.alarabiya.netarticles/2012/02/10/193783 .htm
- Some books that I recommend to read, which contributed to publishing this book:
    1. Dr. Ibrahim al-Faqi, *Negative Thinking and Positive Thinking*. Dar Al- Yaqeen For Publishing & Distribution, Egypt, El Mansoura, 1st edition, 2009.
    2. Dr. Ibrahim al-Faqi, *Human Energy and the Road to the Summit*. Dar Sama For Publishing & Distribution, Egypt.
    3. Dr. Ibrahim Al-Faqi, *Awaken Your Abilities and Make Your Future*. Dar Al- Yaqeen for Publishing and Distribution, Egypt, Mansoura, 2008.
    4. Dr. Ibrahim Al-Faqi, *Life Without Tension*. Dar Sama for Publishing & Distribution, Egypt.
    5. Dr. Ibrahim al-Faqi, *The Ten Keys to Success*. Dar Al- Yaqeen for publication and distribution, Egypt - Mansoura, 2009.
    6. Dr. Ibrahim Al-Faqi, *The Power of Love and Tolerance*. Dar Sama for publication and Distribution, Egypt.
    7. Dr. Ibrahim Al-Faqi *The Art of Serving Scientists and How to Maintain Them*. Bedaya Foundation for Production, Publishing and Distribution, Egypt.

www.ingramcontent.com/pod-product-compliance
Lightning Source LLC
Chambersburg PA
CBHW051842250726
48659CB00005B/1972